POETRY

AND

NATIONAL   CHARACTER

POETRY

AND

NATIONAL CHARACTER

THE LESLIE STEPHEN LECTURE

DELIVERED AT CAMBRIDGE ON 13 MAY 1915

BY

W. MACNEILE DIXON

Professor of English Language and Literature in the
University of Glasgow

Cambridge:
at the University Press
1915

CAMBRIDGE
UNIVERSITY PRESS

University Printing House, Cambridge CB2 8BS, United Kingdom

Published in the United States of America by Cambridge University Press, New York

Cambridge University Press is part of the University of Cambridge.

It furthers the University's mission by disseminating knowledge in the pursuit of
education, learning and research at the highest international levels of excellence.

www.cambridge.org
Information on this title: www.cambridge.org/9781107691445

© Cambridge University Press 1915

First published 1915
First paperback edition 2014

A catalogue record for this publication is available from the British Library

ISBN 978-1-107-69144-5 Paperback

POETRY AND NATIONAL CHARACTER

"THERE are times," wrote Leslie Stephen, "when we feel that we would rather have the actual sounds, the downright utterance of an agonised human being than the far away echo of passion set up in the artistic brain.... We tire of the skilfully prepared sentiment, the pretty fancies, the unreal imaginations, and long for the harsh, crude substantial fact, the actual utterance of men struggling in the dire grasp of unmitigated realities." Such a desire would be satisfied to-day, for we stand in the grasp of these realities; and perhaps nothing is, perhaps nothing should be further from our thoughts than matters of literature and art, "the pretty fancies, the unreal imaginations." Our "forward youth," as in Marvell's Ode, have at their country's call forsaken the "Muses dear," and left the "books in dust" to "oil the unused armour's rust." How faint and faded appear the old academic interests, how unwillingly we concern ourselves with the shadows of the imagined past while our living countrymen challenge by their deeds the heroic records of their forefathers. Happy, indeed, we dare not call these times, yet many a poet, no doubt, many a romancer to come will celebrate them, it may be with that touch of regret that accompanies the chronicle of famous days, the inevitable touch of regret that they are gone. Happier, they may say, those who had a share in the deeds, happier they may even call us, who are warmed by their generous contagion, than our successors born too late to do more than recall and glorify them.

Yet here at Cambridge, although a university so famous in science as to be almost unconscious of its indisputable supremacy in poetry, here one may at any time speak of poetry openly and without apology. Here too, if anywhere, one may appropriately enquire what light our knowledge of English national character throws upon English poetry, or our knowledge of the poetry upon the national character. Such an enquiry aims, indeed, at no final or scientific truth, a mere "sally of the mind" it can only support itself upon the tide of its own interest, but at least it proceeds from a fixed point. However far apart or incompatible they may at times appear some connexion between a nation's character and its poetry there must be.

Imagine for a moment an intelligent foreigner—the witness so readily summoned in such investigations—fairly acquainted with a thousand years of our history, the political and commercial activities of the English race, its religious movements, its wars and colonial enterprises, acquainted with all this but unacquainted with our literature. Would he in turning his attention to that literature instinctively expect it to be supreme in poetry, would he anticipate meeting Shakespeare? Or again, would

he find more of the England he had already
studied, its essential spirit and genius, in
Beowulf, in Chaucer, or in Pope? In his
search for that spirit may one not fancy
him puzzled by the variety in our poetic
moods, by finding Marlowe of the same race
as Cowper, or Dryden as Shelley? All are
Englishmen, but would they appear to have
anything save their language in common?
Whatever the fundamental qualities of a
race may be, and they are neither easily
discovered nor stated, such a student could
hardly, I fancy, deny that we were a practical and at the same time a poetical folk,
or, if not poetical in grain, at least successful in the production of remarkable poetry,
a pleasant inconsistency. Possibly he might
express surprise at such poetic fertility in
an unexpected quarter, in a people obviously
of a practical but not obviously of a poetic
temper. Certainly he would not ascribe
this success to a widely diffused or excep-
tional artistic sense. Of hideous practicality,
of wintry utilitarianism we have often been

accused, but no one has ever yet described the Englishman as a born artist. His amiable tolerance of the artistically intolerable, how unassailable, how triumphant it is! And for supremacy in the plastic arts, no one, I suppose, would turn to England or any northern nation. They are of the South. In these arts races nourished in the Mediterranean tradition alone have succeeded supremely, races in touch with the gorgeous East, educated through the ancient trade routes before the dawn of history by Assyria and Babylon in the values of form, the values of colour, and under skies where form took its sharpest outlines and colour its purest tones. Nobody in the world thinks of the Englishman as a born artist; does anyone think of him as a born poet? Yet the poetry is there. Matthew Arnold, in his famous and engaging discourses at Oxford, explained its presence by dwelling on the Celtic element in the English nature. We were a mixed people, fortunately blended, and the Celt in us resolved the mystery. He it was who redeemed our race from Germanism, gave to our poetry its sense for style and made Shakespeare and Milton possible. This admirable speculation seems to stand where it did, for the ethnologists have not yet convinced each other, and the rest of us can but continue to speculate. The pursuit of certainty is most fascinating in studies that least permit of it, but we still must echo Arnold's cry—"And we then, what are we? what is England?" The hour certainly befriends the Celtic theory, for it seems likely that we shall henceforth count ourselves even less Teutonic than we used to believe, and readily, all of us, become Britons or Normans. If, however, our literary history is made in some ways more intelligible by thinking of the Celt, the rest of our history is made less intelligible by thinking of him. *They went forth to the war, but they always fell* will hardly serve as a sentence to illumine English history. And the talent for affairs, for political compromise, for colonial enterprise—these, I suppose, we must ascribe to the Normans, and it would seem, then, that, by some ingenious division of labour, to the descendants of one race Nature had entrusted the poetic, and to those of another the practical business of the nation. The hypothesis, charming though it be, awaits verification. So rapidly, too, have the researches of the linguistic scholars been succeeded by those of the anthropologists that for races of whom Arnold had never heard a share may yet be claimed in our national achievements. Meanwhile to lay an exact finger upon the contribution of any race to our national history is too hazardous a venture, and it seems preferable to proceed in a simpler fashion, to connect our poetry more directly with English character and history as we know them.

The governing characteristics of the Englishman are not greatly in dispute. His sturdy nationalism, for example, has all along and everywhere been acknowledged. The earliest proof of it lies in the 'withdrawal,' to use Bishop Creighton's word, the 'withdrawal' of England from that marvellous fraternity of the Middle Ages, feudal and Catholic Europe. By the fourteenth century she had become a separate nation, committed to the voyage of her own destiny. At a price the Englishman purchased his freedom. Deliberately he stood aloof from the centre, from the main stream of ideas, from the light and warmth of European civility. He remained, as it were, the country cousin of the family, preferring, one might say, the rough, free out-of-doors life to the elegance and refinements with the accompanying restraints of the town. He declined the advantages of the best Latin society. Unattracted by the mediaeval vision of a united Christendom, of races held together by common acceptance of the same laws, the same religious creeds and observances, the same chivalric ideals, he set over against the abstract perfections of this dazzling scheme his own liberty, his own habits, his own interests. He had no eye for the beauty of a universal, an ideal order. His talent has ever been for life rather than logic. Of general principles because they tend to imprison the individual he is suspicious. "My case is always a special case. Why should I be treated as one of a number, I, who am unlike all the rest?" He preferred, too, the old "laws of St Edward" to any legislative novelties, his own priests and bishops to foreigners, his own language to Norman French. He knew his mind and achieved his ends, not indeed so much by way of argument as by patient indifference to argument, and the gradual development of national consciousness only stiffened his original prejudices. His country satisfied him as the best, his race as manifestly the bravest and the handsomest in the world. To go his own way, think his own thoughts, conduct his own undertakings is all an Englishman asks, or used to ask, and if he interferes in the

affairs of others, it is only that he may
not be interfered with. By this early withdrawal from the comity of European nations,
England led the van in liberty but brought
up the rear in civility. For while they
advanced in the social arts, in literary and
artistic sense, while they seized upon and
familiarised themselves with Renaissance
ideals, she continued to pour her best
energies into practical channels, fighting
within her own borders to lay the founda-
tions of civil liberty and on all the seas
to secure her commercial and yet unseen
imperial future.

The career of Milton illustrates the
national character, its practical and positive
quality. If ever an Englishman was a born
artist, it was he. Yet perceiving on his
Italian journey that, in his own words, " a
way was opening for the establishment of
real liberty," he is at once aroused, forgoes
his studies, abandons his Muse, sacrifices
all his ambitions, and gives the best years
of his life to the cause of political freedom.

How characteristically English that is! This then, as Cardinal Newman said, is "the people for private enterprise," and a little later added with equal truth, "a government is their natural foe." In his private capacity the Englishman owes nothing to the state, he asks nothing from it, he hardly cares for its protection.

> Their governors they count such dangerous things
> That 'tis their custom to affront their kings.

The less government the better has been his consistent creed, for the weaker the central authority the wider field for his own energy and talent. The conviction that the state was made for Englishmen and not Englishmen for the state made it at times his unwilling servant; he was careful that it should never be his master. And the empire? Nothing of course could be further from the truth than to ascribe either its origin or growth to the organised and sustained effort of any central authority. Neither planned for nor foreseen it is, as

Newman so eloquently describes, the work
of individuals, men acting for the most
part without other warrant than their own
energetic inclinations—merchants, travellers,
explorers, adventurers, colonists — whose
unauthorised and personal enterprises,
multitudinous, daring, resourceful, contri-
buted without conscious design to the
astonishing consummation. The state, so
far from encouraging often disowned or
disclaimed responsibility for these individual
performances, and when it lent them support, did so with reluctant tardiness. Is
it surprising that such unconsidered empire-
building appears to exasperate and bewilder
nations accustomed to act only through their
organised authorities, nations which move
in drilled and disciplined masses at the
command of their rulers towards a goal
foreseen and predetermined?

We have then this withdrawal from the
centre and this ineradicable independence as
facts in our political history. Turn to our
literary history and what do we find? That

here too the Englishman went his own way.
One cannot of course picture him as a recluse,
as so aloof and wrapped up in himself as to
refuse all intercourse with his neighbours,
or concern with their ideas. The truth
that by this very withdrawal, this aloofness
he rendered himself very susceptible to the
influence of these ideas when they reached
him. And at seasons they did reach him,
borne across the straits like strange perfumes,
all the charm of social grace and refinement,
of literature and learning and the arts. The
country cousin, of whom I spoke, rarely a
visitor to town, finds its fashions none the
less novel and attractive on that account.
Yet in the main he goes his own way, a
contented rustic. As Pope puts it

> We, brave Britons, foreign laws despised
> And kept unconquer'd and uncivilis'd.

Doubtless, for example, the advocates of
the ancient rules, as recommended to the
Elizabethan playwrights by the elegant and
accomplished Sir Philip Sidney, had the

best of the argument. The English case
remained for long, at least, without defenders.
Yet the dramatists, Shakespeare among them,
continued to write plays which were "neither
right tragedies nor right comedies, mingling
kings and clowns," observing the "rules neither
of honest civility nor of skilful poetry...faulty
both in place and time, the two necessary
companions of all corporal actions." Thus,
as might be expected, the country cousin
has, as Sidney called our drama, "an un-
mannerly daughter showing a bad education."
Doubtless also the quantitative metres so
persuasively urged upon Spenser by his
friend Gabriel Harvey had much to be said
for them. "I like your late Englishe hexa-
meters so exceedingly well," wrote Spenser,
"that I also enure my pen sometime in that
kinde." Yes, but he writes *The Faerie Queene*
in stanzas. The poet Campion is not only
convinced of the superiority of the classical
metres, he is enthusiastic about them, and
produces a treatise in their favour to con-
vince others. But for himself he is careful

not to follow whither the argument leads. He is an Englishman, he turns his back upon it, his practice is better than his theory, and he composes verses, none more charming, that are ruled by rime and accent. Or take the matter of an academy. "It imputes no little disgrace to our Nation," wrote Richard Carew in 1605, "that others have so many Academyes, and wee none at all." Such was also the opinion of Edmund Bolton, whose society, had it been founded in 1616, planned to include great names, Chapman and Drayton and Ben Jonson. Dryden too favoured the design when revived in 1664, Evelyn spoke up for it in a letter to Pepys, Bishop Sprat urged it again in 1667, and Swift in 1712. Admirable reasons were advanced for the project which never lacked friends, yet without opposition it withered, nor does the cause of its ill-success clearly emerge until Dr Johnson set it forth half a century later in his uncompromising fashion. What is the root of his objection? Simply that the less government we have the better, in literature as in politics. "It was a proposal," said he, "which I, who can never wish to see dependence multiplied, hope the spirit of English liberty will hinder or destroy."

As for the profits of this independence, this "spirit of English liberty," we may claim with some confidence that it preserved, in full vigour and vitality, the originality, the genius native to the race. Whatever the dangers of contact with more facile, more fluent, more subtile, more social peoples, these were avoided. In many ways they were real enough. "The Englishman Italianate is the devil incarnate" ran the Elizabethan proverb. "Our countrymen usually bring three things with them out of Italy," it was said, "a naughty conscience, an empty purse, and a weak stomach." If the country cousin escaped moral he escaped also intellectual dangers, too close an imitation, too slavish a pursuit of Latin graces and refinements. This, too, we may claim, and with great assurance, that in trusting to their own

experiences and reflexions our poets and
men of letters drew upon the only authentic
sources of inspiration, and that the strength
of our poetry is due to this trust. The best
school for poetry as for everything else is the
school of personal experience. We may say
with truth that the fortune of our literature
was made by attendance on this school, we
may praise our writers for their originality
and variety, but there are other qualities
for which we cannot praise them. Too
frequently they lack, and our most friendly
critics complain of it, restraint, lucidity,
finish, shapeliness. Allow that inspiration
is less frequently wanting, yet he who trusts
to inspiration, one discovers, too often trusts
to improvisation, and how much of our poetry
is little better than improvisation. And so
foreign critics speak, to our surprise, of " the
rude but splendid Muse of the Britons." If
we expect from a book that it should partake
of the character of a work of art—and we
should expect it—that it should resemble
a picture or a statue, a chapel rather than

an outhouse or barn, then we require a finished product which excludes the ill-considered, the irrelevant, the haphazard; we require a respect for words, we ask that it should avoid verbosity and save our time. But, if we look for these qualities, how often English books disappoint us. And when posterity, most inexorable of critics, gets to work, the evidence for inspiration must indeed be overwhelming if inspiration be asked to excuse verbosity and shapelessness. Our literature has developed in conformity with our national character and we must take what it gives us. It has given us, for example, the novel, the most modern of literary forms, in which we have been specially prolific. How congenial is the novel to our temperament! Here there are no restraints, no laws have been prescribed for its government; it revels in freedom, exalts sentiment, rejoices in the diffuse, despises verbal economy and achieves the very perfection of the amorphous. I do not know how it may be with others, but I find myself constantly in agreement with the sentiment of Amiel: "Keep your vats, your must, your dregs to yourselves: I want wine fully made, wine which will sparkle in the glass."

To return to my thesis. An instinct for emancipation, for a free passage everywhere appears clearly in our literature as in our national character, so that we are and have always been willing to pardon anything to genius, to trust to its happy moments, to overlook its vagaries, to permit every man to be a law unto himself. The apparition of Shakespeare, who never blotted a line, blinds us to the virtues of restraint, of exactness, of order, virtues which, but for our insularity and withdrawal from close contact with Latin culture, might at a price have been ours. Our history shows that above all things we prize originality and independence of mind, that we prize even the eccentric as evidence of spontaneity and truth to nature. We delight in these qualities and are correspondingly indifferent to the disciplined and deliberate

side of art. Nothing so charmed the spectators of Elizabethan tragedy as the exalted,
the towering in character, the superman like
Marlowe's Tamburlaine, storming across the
stage to the capture of Babylon in a chariot
drawn by conquered kings, Caesar, who
bestrode "this narrow world like a Colossus,"
or Antony in whose livery "walk'd crowns
and crownets." Nothing so charmed the
spectators of comedy as the extravagant,
the unconventional in character or person,
the vast bulk and uncontrollable exuberance
of Falstaff, the whimsicalities of Touchstone.
It is their humours we prize in men, not the
qualities which unite but the idiosyncrasies
which distinguish them from each other.
We prefer a parti-coloured world. Nor is
ugliness excluded. That is tolerable, even
welcome, provided it be expressive of indi-
viduality. So much so, indeed, that with us
an author may flourish on his very infirmities.
Why eliminate what unfailingly attracts an
audience? This preference has persisted
with us, and will probably continue to persist.

Not only are we content to be pleased we "know not why and care not wherefore," not only do many of our most talented authors, like Browning, for example, in his *Ring and the Book*, or Mr Hardy in his *Dynasts*, works of genius if you will, make these shapeless, verbose things, but we are satisfied with them and praise them. We must all gladly suffer in the cause of freedom, nothing is so well worth suffering for, but may we not, now and again perhaps, confess to our sufferings, may we not, claiming an English privilege, complain that we pay a high price for it ?

"The world that I regard," said Sir Thomas Browne, "is myself." There again we have the characteristic note. He owns no other authority. "What do I think and feel," he asks, "what shall I do?" not "What are the thoughts, feelings, susceptibilities, what are the counsels of other men ? " Goethe in his conversations with Eckermann praised the English for their courage in being themselves, in following out the bent of their natures. He praised, too, "their ease and confidence among foreigners, as if they were lords everywhere and the whole world belonged to them." Times have changed and Goethe's countrymen no longer praise these qualities. They have ceased to be English virtues and have become English vices. Still, whatever they are, whether virtues or vices, they remain national characteristics. When he writes, our foreign critics assure us, the Englishman gives the impression that he is wholly preoccupied with his own thoughts and feelings, and expresses them first and last for his own satisfaction. "In London," said an eighteenth century Frenchman, "everyone assumes just what character he pleases; there you surprise no one by being yourself." When he turns author he does not change. Men of other and more sociable nations may write to delight or persuade their readers, the Englishman writes that he may converse with himself. He wishes to contemplate his own image in the mirror, to paint, as it were, his own portrait. Clearly in this undertaking a man has less need to imitate others, to consider the example of others, the less need, that is, to follow the rules, the tradition. For what is the tradition? What is it but the body of doctrine, accepted by previous writers, taking stock of earlier successes and failures? Tradition in any art is nothing more than the capitalised experience of its students. If, then, we write to please or persuade others the value of the tradition is evident: it professes to show just how this success may be achieved. If on the other hand we write to please ourselves it is much less evident, for who can guide us to this result better than our own inclinations?

Respect for the tradition, for the opinion of others made French civilisation the wonder and admiration of the world. In French literature deference to authority, regard for the universal, sympathy with the wishes and susceptibilities of men at large, a care for social requirements meet us at every turn. It charms by putting every one of us at his ease, by asking our good opinion, by taking trouble to meet us half way, by introducing us to the pleasant society of like-minded neighbours. If ever writers could say that they "only give back to the public what they had borrowed from it," remarks **M.** Brunetière, French writers may say so. English writers on the other hand borrow nothing from the public, everything from themselves.

I do not for the moment attempt to sum up the gains and losses. This much appears certain. With less respect for the tradition, less for the rules, with a far less sensitive artistic conscience the Englishman was somehow more successful in poetry. He yields to his brilliant neighbours in some but not in all, not even, it would appear, in the most essential points. Where art is faulty there may be insight, and vision, a greater thing, may outrange social sense. Still so valuable is tradition, the body of educated opinion, that without it even genius is almost powerless. To protect oneself against false prophets, against intellectual charlatans, even against clap-trap and fustian is not an easy matter. The intellectual atmosphere is always thick with confused ideas, blurred images, incoherent emotions. Against a man who stands alone false standards will almost certainly prevail. When we stand together, one generation with another, we are in less danger of mistaking for excellence what is far from excellence, of becoming the dupes of temporary fashion. Our national horror of pedantry, of ink-horn terms is justifiable, but respect for the tradition is not pedantry. Without it and the institutions which preserve it how precarious would be our intellectual balance. Our universities and learned societies have no more important function than to protect the nation from a belief in the second-rate, the inferior men and inferior products.

Poetry, least of all arts and sciences, one is accustomed to think, demands knowledge and technical equipment. Poets, we imagine, are happy and irresponsible beings, directed by divine instinct, fortunately free from the dire necessity of preparation or labour imposed upon other men. Wholly guided by inspiration little, we suppose, can be done for them, they are born not made. Yet call to mind the eminent names. Observe how seldom even in this region, sacred to genius, the impulses of inspiration suffice. Few indeed have been the English poets who reached without a guide the summits of fame, few who were not studious disciples of their predecessors, few even, explain it as you please, who were unsupported by a prosaic university education or its equivalents. It would be as vain to seek, we are nevertheless agreed, for the secret of our success in poetry in a regard for the rules of art, the body of received opinion, as in a native or deep-seated sense of beauty. And in truth if poetry were primarily a matter of art, or again if it were the offspring of wit and the social sense, English success in it would be inexplicable. But, say what some critics will, it is not primarily a matter of art at all. One cannot enter the temple, as Plato said, by the help of art. No, we may answer, nor yet without it.

Briefly, let us say, success in poetry is attained when finished and arresting expression is given to some moving thought or experience. We must look for it, therefore, where thought and word, inspiration and art are found together, at a confluence of streams. It will be found, I believe, chiefly in our history when in the traffic of thought the intellect of one race meets the intellect of another, at the moments of their most fruitful union.

There have been many definitions of poetry. From among them let me take Newman's. Poetry, said Newman, is " originality energising in the world of beauty." By common consent the English have been distinguished by their originality and energy. History shows, indeed, how much of their energy was devoted to the preservation or protection of this originality, how jealously the right to exercise it was guarded. Originality and energy are there, native to them, splendid and conspicuous talents. But the talent for beauty, the sense for

beauty, like that of the Greeks pervading
the whole of life, the extreme sensitiveness
to every breath of loveliness whether in nature
or language or art, that talent and that
sensitiveness we can claim neither for our
ancestors nor for ourselves. The sense for
beauty is not native to us and needs kindling.
For this, if for no other reason, the study
of Greek literature and art, where we are
at the fountain head of beauty, should be
of all literatures and arts the most precious
to our countrymen. But, if a sense of beauty
be not native to us, an essential element as
required in Newman's definition is lacking.
The sense needs, as I have said, kindling,
and if for the flame that kindled it we go
in search among the constituent races that
produced " that heterogeneous thing an
Englishman," we plunge into the unknown,
we elaborate a speculative psychology. If
one says "England is England and France
is France " one is clearly enough understood,
but in attempting to penetrate far behind
these terms nothing is easier than to lose

one's footing. Attempting to pass behind the term 'England' Matthew Arnold could see no brilliant prospect for our poetry in the characteristics of the Anglo-Saxon, and quotes the old Irish poem which derides him—"For dullness the creeping Saxons." He turned, therefore, as we have seen, to the Celt and put his trust in Celtic romance and love of beauty. Possibly he was right, but without committing ourselves to a perilous decision here, let us take a stand on firmer ground, on the notion of the crossing of ideas rather than of races, the fertilisation, if we may call it so, of one type of genius by another type.

By withdrawal from the closer intimacy offered her with Latin civilisation England preserved nationality, point of view, the distinctive flavour of her own qualities. She preserved originality, and the flood of native energy, derived from many tributary races, flowed into a thousand practical channels. While to her southern neighbours England seemed the fitting home of

a restless melancholy people, inhabiting a
country of pale sunshine, blurred landscapes
and unwilling soil, a clumsy people, unlet-
tered, mannerless, made " terrible and bold,"
as Defoe said, by their climate, but otherwise
negligible, she was far from intellectually
idle. So late as the seventeenth century
Louis XIV asked whether there existed any
writers or scholars in England. Yet in
truth for centuries, unassisted, untutored
by ancient sages, guided mainly by their
own instincts the English had for themselves
faced the old human problems. Thrown
upon their native resources they had been,
and were not ill-content to be their own
prophets and teachers, their own philoso-
phers. Though so late in history, with
ancient civilisations behind them, never very
closely in touch with these civilisations, they
encountered the world with virgin minds.
Nor is it wonderful that so occupied they
placed life before art. Our pre-Norman
literature, like *Beowulf,* harsh and untutored
though it be, is firmly rooted in experience.

How clearly it sees life for what it is and how fearlessly meets it! It faces the world with a philosophy unborrowed from books and yet perfectly suited to that world. Compare *Beowulf* with Homer, and you may safely claim Homer's superiority in beauty and poetic quality, not so safely his superiority in masculine vigour and truth. "Better it is that a man should avenge his friend than that he should greatly mourn. Every one of us comes to his end, let him who will achieve renown, leaving a famous name." "Not a foot's length shall I give back before the warden of the barrow, but it shall be for us at the rampart as fate, the disposer of all men, may decree." Who is speaking here? One might fancy Homer himself. Or at a later date compare Dante and Langland, visionaries both, not far separated from each other in time. Where does the Englishman yield to the Italian? Yield to him he must at every point of art, grace, finish, sweetness, dignity. Yet assuredly half barbaric as he seems, a wild

and rugged figure beside the learned and
aristocratic Dante, Langland is not less
impressive in his fiery intensity, in his un-
yielding grasp of realities. Of his own
world he is as complete a master, nor does
a feature of it escape him. He knows his
England and probes it to the quick, but
the world of beauty he never enters. That
is where Langland fails as a poet. Where
there is no beauty there is no poetry. That
is where his countryman and contemporary
Chaucer so magnificently succeeds. Chaucer
succeeds because his eyes have been opened
to another vision. Over against the imper-
fections of the world of humanity he per-
ceived the perfections of the world of
art. He had been, we may say, at school
in France and at the university in Italy.
Yet if poetry is not fundamentally a matter
of art but a matter of mental and emotional
experiences, and of the variety and intensity
of these experiences, this preoccupation with
life may prove the best preparation for it.
Then any man who has adventured far on

this voyage, who loves, in Chapman's phrase, "to have his sails filled with a lusty wind," who has been moved and thrilled by the great spectacle is potentially a poet. And what strikes one in comparing our own with the poetry of any other modern nation, the last five centuries of our literature with that of Spain, of France or of Italy, is the wealth and variety of its themes. Their themes are on the whole slighter and fewer, their poetry has its roots in love and war, in romantic subjects generally, and is far less occupied with the whole range of human experience than ours. English writers have forced, we might say, more of the prose of life to become poetry. They have gathered the "pleasant honey of the Muses" where flowers seemed least abundant. They have usually escaped too, so intent are they upon the main issues of thought, that last poetic infirmity, the elaborate chasing of the cup that contains nothing. Rarely have they offered us wine without body. What thoughts have not passed through the minds of these men, what feelings have they not experienced? How vast the field touched with emotion is there, how many characters studied, humours explored, speculations pursued, passions expressed! How varied, in a word, the mental energy and activity they display. Shakespeare, its greatest author, is typical of our literature at large. Not without faults of taste, never sure-footed even in his finest passages, he yet easily eclipses all others in the breadth of his human interests. Shakespeare is what he is, one need have no reservations in saying it, not as an artist but as a citizen of the world. True to his race he never shows himself anxious about the rules, but rejoicing in freedom reviews the length and breadth of existence and stretches out his rod from pole to pole of human nature. There is nothing accidental in this, he pursues the curve determined by his English bias.

Everywhere then our writers are observers

and thinkers first and poets afterwards. When they fail it is because they are without wings, never because they are without ideas. Take Chaucer, who was, as I have said, at school in France and at the university in Italy. In him the English genius flowered when the observant, reflective spirit, which had explored human experience, met the genius of the South and had revealed to it the persuasive charm of form and symmetry, of rhythm and order and the craft of words. So with the "new company of courtly-makers" in the sixteenth century: "they travelled into Italy," says Puttenham, "and there tasted the sweet and stately measures and style of the Italian poesy." In our history success in poetry is met with where a current of ideas not distinctively English flows into the main stream of national thought and disturbs it. From the ripples and eddies that are then formed, from the agitation and disquiet we judge the presence of a new force. In the ferment created by the clashing of opposites, under the stimulus of unfamiliar emotions the originality and energy of the English spirit blossoms, the sturdy tree of independent thought puts forth flower and fruit. At every point where our poetry rises to great elevations the native strain is crossed by another. Tempering its gravity with extreme sweet the high austere soul of Spenser looks out from a palace of splendours, the voluptuous splendours of intoxicating Italy. In Marlowe England meets full face the gale of Renaissance passions. The shining perfection of Greek art passed like an arrow through the harness of Milton's Puritanism. To Dryden and Pope the exquisite shapeliness, the logic and precision required by the French spirit flung an unceasing challenge. From "the horns of Elfland" strange airs floated to the ears of Gray and his successors.

But some one will say, how comes it that the distinction of English literature is not in prose rather than poetry? The mind of a practical and energetic people accustomed to take what is offered, to deal directly with the matter in hand, will express itself more naturally and completely in a plain and simple fashion, the fashion of prose, rather than in a heightened and elaborate fashion, the fashion of poetry. It will be more at its ease in the field of reason than of imagination. Yet we know the opposite to be the truth. Practical and lovers of freedom as they are, revolting against all checks and limitations, English writers have been somehow assisted by the very checks and limitations which poetry imposes. Its strictness helps rather than hinders them. Wordsworth, to take a striking example, was helped not hindered by the boundaries of the sonnet. The more the stream of his thought was confined within banks, the less it was permitted to overflow into unrestricted areas, the more powerful became the current. And what is true of Wordsworth is true of English writers in general. Is Shakespeare less effective in his sonnets, or less effective in

the plays where he permits himself least
freedom, than elsewhere in his works? No
one will say so. But that is not all. English
thought in a surprising and surpassing
measure associates itself with emotion. I
shall not here ask the interesting question,
how far it is possible to think without feeling
at the same time, how far what one may
describe as pure thinking can be conducted
at all, thinking, that is, largely or altogether
disentangled or dissociated from feeling.
Setting aside this fascinating question we
may assert that with us more of emotion
enters into our thinking than with most
other peoples, we throw the whole of our
natures, as it were, into the process, which
is, with us, not an excited or rapid, but a
robust one. We do not think so lucidly and
logically as the French. Everyone must
acknowledge the French superiority in that
respect. Yet because our thought is more
highly charged with feeling it is the richer
in consequence. It is obscurer but more
glowing, less exact because more luxuriant.

And our poetry profits by it. Indeed since poetry for most of its lovers provides confused delight rather than a pure intellectual pleasure, we are the better fitted to excel in it. Poetry, said Coleridge, with great acuteness, "gives more pleasure when only generally and not perfectly understood." The mood of poetry is never the logical or analytic mood, never the mood in which we approach the investigation of truth, but always that in which we enjoy some accepted truth. And even our prose writers, so continuously is their thought accompanied and supported by feeling, are rarely capable of presenting a subject in the dry cool light of the isolated intelligence. Our best prose, as the critics frequently inform us, is imaginative, inspired by sympathy with its subject, by warmth of heart rather than by the spirit of scientific enquiry.

Thus then the connexion between our national character and the achievements of our poets may partly be traced. And what may we conclude? We may conclude

in the first place that to nothing as a people
do we owe so much as to the spirit of liberty,
the soul, as it were, of our national life.
Everywhere and at all times it has inspired
and directed our activities. We do not
exist as a nation in order to excel in any
one respect, to make ourselves powerful,
or artistic or anything else. We prefer to
leave a wide field for the development of
all forms and types of excellence; not by
the subordination of the rest to compass
any one end, but rather to keep open the
avenues to many. As a people we are for
excluding no quality for the sake of another,
exalting no single virtue as super-excellent
or final. It is not in our nature to enslave
ourselves for scientific method or artistic
success or military strength. We wish, and
we are constantly blamed for it, to be
men rather than professionals or specialists,
whether artists, savants or soldiers. We
place the possession of freedom before all
other aims. In its defence we have made
many sacrifices in the past and are prepared

to make further sacrifices. So precious a
thing must be preserved at all costs. But
we must also conclude that whether in life
or literature freedom has its dangers. In
the field of foreign politics, for example,
as our present situation proves, a free
people is at manifest, in war it may easily
be at a fatal disadvantage. Though pos-
sessed of ample resources it may be
suddenly struck down by an envious rival
organised not so much for peace as for
war, by some nation which is nothing else
than an army ever prepared to strike, a
nation under a strong central government,
ruling as if from the heavens, to which
it is perfectly submissive. "If we prefer to
meet danger with a light heart but without training," said Pericles in addressing
the Athenians, "with a courage which is
gained by habit and not enforced by law,
are we not greatly the gainers?" We
have hitherto held the same view. The
reflexion has, however, been forced upon
us that England is no longer as remote

from Europe as in former times and can no longer withdraw itself from European concerns. As freedom of speech, of criticism, the free exchange of ideas, can alone help us to the best thought, the best ideas, so, if we aspire to lead the world, no other course than to preserve our free political institutions seems open. Yet to play so splendid a rôle is to occupy a dangerous post. Nor will our insular position serve us in the future to pursue our national aims undisturbed as it has served us in the past. In art and literature, too, freedom has its perils. No one who knows our literature will deny this, will deny that it has suffered from disorder and caprice, from obscurity and eccentricity, in a word from too much liberty rather than from too much rigour and formality. If freedom, however, means anything it means tolerance, and if tolerance is to be real we must for the sake of the blessing of liberty, put up with every kind of disagreeable absurdity, with works manifestly in the worst taste, and

ridiculous demands upon us to admire them,
with the personal vagaries of well-intentioned
but ill-educated persons who force themselves
upon our attention, and too often succeed
in capturing the public, in degrading its
judgment and confusing its conscience. In
praising freedom one should remember that
it does not sanctify all that it permits. In
politics freedom such as ours may lead to
ruin unless as a people we retain our
sagacity, good sense enough not to be
imposed upon, not to be hoodwinked; in
art, unless we make habitual reference to
the tradition, the capitalised experience of
the past, it leads to our being in Renan's
phrase "devoured by charlatanism."

What form our political institutions
should take in the future if we are to
preserve our freedom, how we may best
protect it, though an attractive theme, is
here beyond us. But in the world of
letters, limiting ourselves to that, when we
cast our eyes abroad and behold the new
and greater England beyond two oceans,

we should, I think, dwell more upon the qualities in which we are deficient, which we have found difficult of attainment, less upon those natural to us. And that for two reasons. The qualities natural to us need not be insisted upon, they will make their appearance without any conscious effort. Independence of mind, trust in happy inspirations, dislike of formality and pedantry, these characteristics we are not likely to lose. It was for a very brief period in our history that we seemed in danger of preferring Waller to Shakespeare. That is the first, and not a negligible reason, but the second outweighs it. The qualities that come less easily to us have acquired a new value. If, and it seems probable for some time to come, the language of these islands be accepted as the standard, if our writers at home be looked to for guidance by the writers of English abroad, then, whether in prose or poetry, the merits of a scrupulous style demand reconsideration. A style of the centre, less highly charged with personal qualities, marked by its respect for words, its exactness and lucidity, its finish and purity should, to meet the circumstances, rise in our estimation. If our writers aspire to be in any measure the schoolmasters of the English world they must become lovers of restraint and proportion, of shapeliness and verbal economy. The secret way to the reader's heart does not lie through self-indulgence, indifference to form and finish, disdain of discipline and the labour of the file. Nor does the way to permanence lie through them. Emancipation is not everything. Negligence and indolence are too often its accompaniments. Dryden, not the least careful of our authors, was, says Dr Johnson, "no rigid judge of his own pages; he seldom struggled after supreme excellence, but snatched in haste what was within his reach." With such a temper, and it is the English temper, more especially since the torrent of print daily increases in the world, and must still further increase, since we are all writers now, with such a temper we shall have a hard task to protect our language from deterioration and decay. The praise given to Dryden, that he found English poetry brick and left it marble, praise too great even for Dryden, can never again be adjudged to any English poet. The smooth and bright perfection of marble, the substance in which the qualities of the Greek spirit found their exquisite symbol, is beyond the reach of our language and our poetry. The most we can hope for them, and that only if we submit to uncongenial discipline, is the strength and durability of bronze.